BOOK 4

Ruth Miskin

Superphonics

The simplest, fastest way to
teach your child to read

Contents

Hodder
Children's
Books

a division of Hodder Headline

What is meant by the term 'phonics'?

Phonics is a highly effective way of teaching reading and spelling, based on the link between sounds and the way in which we write them down. A unit of sound is called a phoneme (*foe-neem*), and the written version of it is called a grapheme:

c / a / t   contains 3 graphemes and 3 phonemes

ch / a / t   contains 3 graphemes and 3 phonemes

f / l / a / t   contains 4 graphemes and 4 phonemes

Note: A phoneme may contain more than one letter. A letter has a name: *dee*
and a sound: *d (d)*

Letters are divided into 2 groups:
Vowels: *a e i o u*
Consonants: *b c d f g h j k l m n p q r s t v w x y z*

How does *Superphonics* teach this?

There are 5 books in the series. The chart on the inside front cover shows which graphemes/phonemes are taught in each book. Each book builds on the skills already learned, and there are plenty of opportunities for revision and practice.

Each book is divided into units, all of which are organised in the same way.

Each unit in this book and Books 2, 3 and 5 consists of 6 steps:

STEP 1 FIND THE RHYMING WORDS
The ability to rhyme is an important skill. If your child can read and spell *cat*, he or she will be able to read and spell *mat* – and so on.

STEP 2 FIND THE SOUNDS
Now your child is taught to hear the separate phonemes in a word: *c / a / t*. Most children need to be taught that each word is made up of individual sounds. In the game Phoneme Fingers, your child is taught to count the phonemes on his or her fingers.

STEP 3 BLEND THE SOUNDS
The little alien Phoneme Fred is useful here. Poor Phoneme Fred can only speak in separate phonemes – *c / a / t* – and your child will be able to help him to blend these into a spoken word.

STEP 4 SPLIT THE WORD INTO SOUNDS
Hearing the phonemes, and saying them in quick succession, prepares children for spelling.

STEP 5 READ THE WORD
Your child is taught how to read the word phoneme by phoneme, always going from left to right.

STEP 6 SPELL THE WORD
This is a writing activity, in which your child will learn how to turn the phonemes into graphemes, or written letters. Ask your child to read his or her writing back to you.

Some children take time to learn how to write. Don't spend too long on this step, and don't worry if your child's spelling is not developing as quickly as his or her reading.

Phoneme Fred

This is a unit from Book 4.

This text tells you what to do.

This text is 'script' for you to read aloud to your child.

This text is for your child to read. A few words are printed in blue. These are difficult words, or words which contain graphemes which have not yet been taught. You may need to help your child to read these. (Some unfamiliar words, such as *candle*, can be read by sounding out the first few phonemes - *c / a / n* - and guessing the rest from what is already known of the text.) Silent letters, such as the *k* in *know*, are printed in red, to show your child that they are not pronounced.

Helpful hints are printed in boxes like this.

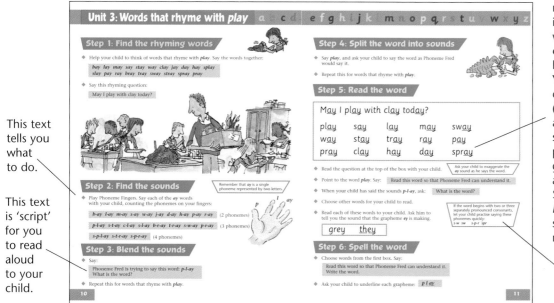

How do I know it will work?

In the author's school, where this method is used, the reading ages of children in Years 2 to 4 are about 2 years higher than their actual ages.

I'm not a teacher – will I be able to do it?

Yes! *Superphonics* is clearly structured and clearly written, in plain English. The 'step' method of working will rapidly become familiar to you and your child.

My life is very busy – how much time will it take up?

If you spend just 20 minutes on *Superphonics* each day, your child will make swift progress. Book 1 will take about 4 weeks, Book 2 will take 2-6 weeks and Books 3-5 will each take 1-2 weeks to complete. If you can't manage 20 minutes every day, don't worry. Just do what you can.

Will I need to collect lots of bits and pieces before we can start?

No! All you need, apart from the books, is a notebook or a few sheets of paper, and a sharp pencil. A small mirror (for looking at mouth shape) is useful but not essential.

Will *Superphonics* enable my child to read stories?

Yes! He or she will be able to read stories, street signs, lists, adverts – and lots more! But don't wait until you have finished *Superphonics* to share books and other kinds of reading.

This book teaches the 'long' vowel sounds:

ay / ey / a-e   *igh / i-e*
ee / e   *ow / o-e / o*   *oo / o*

(Note that *e-e* words such as *here*, and *u-e* words such as *tune*, are not taught as they are not common in English.)

In Book 4, your child should be ready to deal with letter names (*dee*) as well as letter sounds (*d*). He or she may know these names already, perhaps from singing alphabet songs.

Unit 1: Words that rhyme with *sheep*  a b c d

Step 1: Find the rhyming words

◆ Help your child to think of words that rhyme with *sheep*. Say the words together:

> weep sleep deep keep peep creep steep cheep jeep bleep seep sweep beep

◆ Say this rhyming phrase:

> Three sheep in a deep sleep

> Don't worry if your child suggests *ea* words such as *leap*. Explain that there are other ways of spelling the sound.

Step 2: Find the sounds

◆ Say:

> Here is Phoneme Fred, the alien.
> He speaks in sounds, not whole words.

◆ Play Phoneme Fingers. Say each of the *eep* words with your child, counting the phonemes on your fingers:

> Remember that *sh* and *ee* are single phonemes, each represented by two letters.

> sh-ee-p w-ee-p d-ee-p k-ee-p p-ee-p ch-ee-p
> j-ee-p s-ee-p b-ee-p   (3 phonemes)

> s-l-ee-p c-r-ee-p s-t-ee-p b-l-ee-p s-w-ee-p   (4 phonemes)

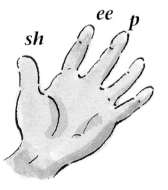

Step 3: Blend the sounds

◆ Say:

> Phoneme Fred is trying to say this word: *sh-ee-p*
> What is the word?

◆ Repeat this for words that rhyme with *sheep*.

Step 4: Split the word into sounds

◆ Say **sheep**, and ask your child to say the word as Phoneme Fred would say it.

◆ Repeat this for words that rhyme with **sheep**.

Step 5: Read the word

> Silent letters are printed in red. Explain to your child that they are not pronounced.

Three sheep in a deep sleep

sheep	bee	feet	heel	feed	been
steep	tree	street	feel	need	seen
keep	knee	sheet	wheel	weed	keen

◆ Read the phrase at the top of the box with your child.

> Ask your child to exaggerate the **ee** sound as he says the word.

◆ Point to the word **sheep**. Say: Read this word so that Phoneme Fred can understand it.

◆ When your child has said the sounds **sh-ee-p**, ask: What is the word?

◆ Choose other words for your child to read, column by column and then at random.

◆ Read each of these words to your child.
Ask him to tell you the sound that the grapheme **e** is making.

> This spelling of the sound **ee** is not used in many words, but the words in which it is used are very common.

he   me   she   we   be

Step 6: Spell the word

◆ Choose words from the first box, column by column and then at random. Say:

Read this word so that Phoneme Fred can understand it.
Write the word.

> Use letter names when talking about graphemes, and letter sounds when talking about phonemes.

◆ Ask your child to underline each grapheme: **w ee p   sh ee p**

5

Step 1: Find the rhyming words

◆ Help your child to think of words that rhyme with **moon**. Say the words together:

> *soon spoon noon goon swoon croon boon*

◆ Say this rhyming sentence:

> A goon on a spoon went to the moon at noon.

Step 2: Find the sounds

◆ Play Phoneme Fingers. Say each of the **oon** words with your child, counting the phonemes on your fingers:

> *m-oo-n s-oo-n n-oo-n g-oo-n b-oo-n*   (3 phonemes)

> *s-p-oo-n s-w-oo-n c-r-oo-n*   (4 phonemes)

Remember that **oo** is a single phoneme represented by two letters.

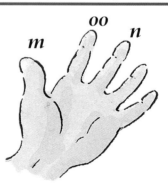

See how quickly your child can count the phonemes on her fingers.

Step 3: Blend the sounds

◆ Say:

> Phoneme Fred is trying to say this word: *m-oo-n*
> What is the word?

◆ Repeat this for words that rhyme with **moon**.

Step 4: Split the word into sounds

- Say *moon*, and ask your child to say the word as Phoneme Fred would say it.

- Repeat this for words that rhyme with *moon*.

Step 5: Read the word

A goon on a spoon went to the moon at noon.

moon	food	school	gloom	shoot
spoon	mood	pool	room	boot
soon	brood	cool	broom	hoot

- Read the sentence at the top of the box with your child.

> Ask your child to exaggerate the *oo* sound as she says the word.

- Point to the word *moon*. Say: Read this word so that Phoneme Fred can understand it.

- When your child has said the sounds *m-oo-n*, ask: What is the word?

- Choose other words for your child to read, column by column and then at random.

- Read each of these words to your child.
  Ask her to tell you the sound that the grapheme *o* is making.

> This spelling of the sound *oo* is not used in many words, but the words in which it is used are very common.

to	do	who

Step 6: Spell the word

- Choose words from the first box, column by column and then at random. Say:

> Read this word so that Phoneme Fred can understand it.
> Write the word.

- Ask your child to underline each grapheme: *m oo n*

ee and oo

◆ Ask your child to read each set of words, emphasising the vowel sound.

sheep	bee	moon	mood
feel	been	boom	soon
seed	meet	school	broom
tree	deep	boot	pool
keen	peel	food	hoot
sweet	deed	spoon	croon
keep	see	room	zoom
heel	green	fool	cool
need	feet	shoot	root

- Tell your child that some of the words learned so far have been mixed up.

- Ask your child to read each word.

sheep	tree	deep	school
mood	sweet	meet	bee
shoot	boom	keep	feel
cool	fool	room	see
heel	food	spoon	keen
broom	been	soon	green
boot	root	pool	deed
need	croon	seed	feet
peel	moon	hoot	zoom

Unit 3: Words that rhyme with *play*

abcd

Step 1: Find the rhyming words

◆ Help your child to think of words that rhyme with **play**. Say the words together:

> *bay lay may say stay way clay jay day hay splay*
> *slay pay ray bray tray sway stray spray pray*

◆ Say this rhyming question:

> May I play with clay today?

Step 2: Find the sounds

Remember that **ay** is a single phoneme represented by two letters.

◆ Play Phoneme Fingers. Say each of the **ay** words with your child, counting the phonemes on your fingers:

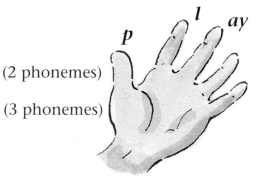

> *b-ay l-ay m-ay s-ay w-ay j-ay d-ay h-ay p-ay r-ay*   (2 phonemes)

> *p-l-ay s-t-ay c-l-ay s-l-ay b-r-ay t-r-ay s-w-ay p-r-ay*   (3 phonemes)

> *s-p-l-ay s-t-r-ay s-p-r-ay*   (4 phonemes)

Step 3: Blend the sounds

◆ Say:

> Phoneme Fred is trying to say this word: **p-l-ay**
> What is the word?

◆ Repeat this for words that rhyme with **play**.

10

Step 4: Split the word into sounds

◆ Say **play**, and ask your child to say the word as Phoneme Fred would say it.

◆ Repeat this for words that rhyme with **play**.

Step 5: Read the word

> # May I pl<u>ay</u> wi<u>th</u> cl<u>ay</u> tod<u>ay</u>?
>
> pl<u>ay</u>   <u>s</u><u>ay</u>   l<u>ay</u>   m<u>ay</u>   sw<u>ay</u>
>
> w<u>ay</u>   st<u>ay</u>   tr<u>ay</u>   r<u>ay</u>   p<u>ay</u>
>
> pr<u>ay</u>   cl<u>ay</u>   h<u>ay</u>   d<u>ay</u>   spr<u>ay</u>

◆ Read the question at the top of the box with your child.

> Ask your child to exaggerate the **ay** sound as he says the word.

◆ Point to the word **play**. Say: Read this word so that Phoneme Fred can understand it.

◆ When your child has said the sounds **p-l-ay**, ask: What is the word?

◆ Choose other words for your child to read.

> If the word begins with two or three separately pronounced consonants, let your child practise saying these phonemes quickly:
> **s-w sw   s-p-r spr**

◆ Read each of these words to your child. Ask him to tell you the sound that the grapheme **ey** is making.

> gr<u>ey</u>   th<u>ey</u>

Step 6: Spell the word

◆ Choose words from the first box. Say:

> Read this word so that Phoneme Fred can understand it.
> Write the word.

◆ Ask your child to underline each grapheme: <u>p l ay</u>

Step 1: Find the rhyming words

◆ Help your child to think of words that rhyme with *cake*. Say the words together:

> bake fake quake drake sake wake make
> take shake lake flake snake rake

◆ Say this rhyming sentence:

> Make a cake, bake a cake, shake a flake on the cake.

Step 2: Find the sounds

In these words, the letters *a* and *e* make a single sound (*ay*), although they are separated by the *k*.

◆ Play Phoneme Fingers. Say each of the *ake* words with your child, counting the phonemes on your fingers:

> c-a-k e b-a-k e f-a-k e qu-a-k e s-a-k e w-a-k e
> m-a-k e t-a-k e sh-a-k e l-a-k e r-a-k e   (3 phonemes)

> d-r-a-k e f-l-a-k e s-n-a-k e   (4 phonemes)

Step 3: Blend the sounds

◆ Say:

> Phoneme Fred is trying to say this word: *c-a-k e*
> What is the word?

◆ Repeat this for words that rhyme with *cake*.

Step 4: Split the word into sounds

◆ Say *cake*, and ask your child to say the word as Phoneme Fred would say it.

◆ Repeat this for words that rhyme with *cake*.

Step 5: Read the word

> Point out the line joining the *a* to the *e* in each word. Tell your child that they are holding hands to make the sound *ay*.

Make a cake, bake a cake, shake a flake on the cake.

cake	made	pane	ate	gave
snake	shade	plane	date	save
take	spade	lane	late	brave

◆ Read the sentence at the top of the box with your child.

> Ask your child to exaggerate the vowel sound as she says the word.

◆ Point to the word *cake*. Say: Read this word so that Phoneme Fred can understand it.

◆ When your child has said the sounds *c-a-k e*, ask: What is the word?

◆ Choose other words for your child to read, column by column and then at random.

> In *ace* words such as *face*, the c is pronounced *s*. In *age* words such as *cage*, the g is pronounced *j*.

Step 6: Spell the word

◆ Choose words from the box, column by column and then at random. Say:

Read this word so that Phoneme Fred can understand it.
Write the word.

◆ Ask your child to underline each grapheme and to join the *a* to the *e* with a line: c a k e

ee, oo, ay and a-e

◆ Ask your child to read each set of words, emphasising the vowel sound.

sheep	moon	play	cake
three	school	may	shade
feet	zoo	bay	brave
feel	food	day	late
teeth	room	tray	same
see	boot	hay	blaze
meet	boo	lay	snake
deep	fool	pay	save
keel	zoom	spray	name

◆ Tell your child that some of the words learned so far have been mixed up.

◆ Ask your child to read each word.

When your child can read the words easily, see how quickly he or she can read them.

tray	sheep	keel	blaze
room	brave	see	snake
boot	may	fool	spray
teeth	school	hay	cake
play	late	boo	zoom
name	day	save	shade
moon	zoo	deep	same
food	feel	pay	three
bay	meet	feet	lay

Unit 5: Words that rhyme with *night*

Step 1: Find the rhyming words

◆ Help your child to think of words that rhyme with **night**. Say the words together:

> light sight might right flight blight plight slight knight bright fright tight

◆ Say this rhyming phrase:

> A bright light at night

Step 2: Find the sounds

◆ Play Phoneme Fingers. Say each of the **ight** words with your child, counting the phonemes on your fingers:

> n-igh-t l-igh-t s-igh-t m-igh-t r-igh-t kn-igh-t t-igh-t   (3 phonemes)

> f-l-igh-t b-l-igh-t p-l-igh-t s-l-igh-t b-r-igh-t f-r-igh-t   (4 phonemes)

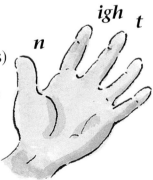

Step 3: Blend the sounds

◆ Say:

> Phoneme Fred is trying to say this word: **n-igh-t**
> What is the word?

◆ Repeat this for words that rhyme with **night**.

Step 4: Split the word into sounds

◆ Say **night**, and ask your child to say the word as Phoneme Fred would say it.

◆ Repeat this for words that rhyme with **night**.

Step 5: Read the word

Remember that **igh** is a single phoneme represented by three letters.

A br<u>igh</u>t l<u>igh</u>t at n<u>igh</u>t

n<u>igh</u>t	m<u>igh</u>t	t<u>igh</u>t	sl<u>igh</u>t
s<u>igh</u>t	r<u>igh</u>t	f<u>igh</u>t	fr<u>igh</u>t

◆ Read the phrase at the top of the box with your child.

Ask your child to exaggerate the **igh** sound as he says the word.

◆ Point to the word **night**. Say: Read this word so that Phoneme Fred can understand it.

◆ When your child has said the sounds **n-igh-t**, ask: What is the word?

◆ Choose other words for your child to read.

◆ Read each of these words to your child.
Ask him to tell you the sound that the grapheme **y** is making.

my	by	<u>sh</u>y	cry	fly	sky

Step 6: Spell the word

◆ Choose words from the first box. Say:

Read this word so that Phoneme Fred can understand it.
Write the word.

◆ Ask your child to underline each grapheme: **<u>n</u> <u>igh</u> <u>t</u>**

Step 1: Find the rhyming words

◆ Help your child to think of words that rhyme with **pine**. Say the words together:

> *nine shrine vine whine swine twine dine fine wine shine spine line mine*

◆ Say this rhyming phrase:

> Nine fine pines in a line

Step 2: Find the sounds

In these words, the letters **i** and **e** make a single sound (**igh**), although they are separated by the **n**.

◆ Play Phoneme Fingers. Say each of the **ine** words with your child, counting the phonemes on your fingers:

> p-i-n e n-i-n e v-i-n e wh-i-n e d-i-n e
> f-i-n e w-i-n e sh-i-n e l-i-n e m-i-n e   (3 phonemes)

> sh-r-i-n e s-w-i-n e t-w-i-n e s-p-i-n e   (4 phonemes)

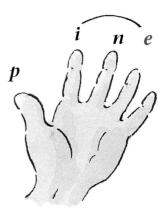

Step 3: Blend the sounds

◆ Say:

> Phoneme Fred is trying to say this word: **p-i-n e**
> What is the word?

◆ Repeat this for words that rhyme with **pine**.

Step 4: Split the word into sounds

◆ Say **pine**, and ask your child to say the word as Phoneme Fred would say it.

◆ Repeat this for words that rhyme with **pine**.

Step 5: Read the word

Point out the line joining the **i** to the **e** in each word. Tell your child that they are holding hands.

Nine fine pines in a line

pine	ride	life	mile
mine	slide	wife	tile
shine	stride	knife	while
time	mice	kite	five
crime	slice	write	live
slime	twice	quite	dive

◆ Read the phrase at the top of the box with your child.

Ask your child what sound the letter **c** is making in **mice, slice and twice**.

◆ Point to the word **pine**. Say: Read this word so that Phoneme Fred can understand it.

◆ When your child has said the sounds **p-i-n e**, ask: What is the word?

◆ Choose other words for your child to read, column by column and then at random.

Step 6: Spell the word

◆ Choose words from the box, column by column and then at random. Say:

Read this word so that Phoneme Fred can understand it.
Write the word.

◆ Ask your child to underline each grapheme and to join the **i** to the **e** with a line: p i n e

ee, oo, ay, a-e, igh and i-e

◆ Ask your child to read each set of words, emphasising the vowel sound.

sheep	moon	play
feet	fool	day
three	soon	tray
street	broom	pay
wheel	school	may
seed	zoom	stay
cake	night	pine
snake	bright	size
gate	sight	slide
safe	light	white
spade	tight	shine
date	fright	site

◆ Tell your child that some of the words learned so far have been mixed up.

◆ Ask your child to read each word.

sheep	night	slide	stay
bright	zoom	wheel	pine
day	soon	tray	snake
date	sight	seed	pay
play	fool	shine	light
site	cake	may	broom
safe	size	tight	school
white	gate	feet	moon
spade	fright	three	street

Step 1: Find the rhyming words

◆ Help your child to think of words that rhyme with **snow**. Say the words together:

> *slow low blow grow throw glow flow mow know crow show tow stow*

◆ Say this rhyming sentence:

> I know a crow who likes to blow snow.

> Don't worry if your child suggests *ough* words such as *dough*, or *oe* words such as *toe*.

Step 2: Find the sounds

> Some *ow* words, such as **crown**, are pronounced differently. (See Book 5.)

◆ Play Phoneme Fingers. Say each of the **ow** words with your child, counting the phonemes on your fingers:

> *l-ow m-ow kn-ow sh-ow t-ow*   (2 phonemes)

> *s-n-ow s-l-ow b-l-ow g-r-ow th-r-ow*
> *g-l-ow f-l-ow c-r-ow s-t-ow*   (3 phonemes)

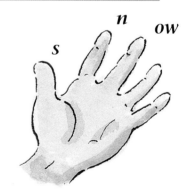

Step 3: Blend the sounds

◆ Say:

> Phoneme Fred is trying to say this word: *s-n-ow*
> What is the word?

> Some *ow* words have two meanings and can be pronounced in two ways: *bow, sow, row*.

◆ Repeat this for words that rhyme with **snow**.

Step 4: Split the word into sounds

◆ Say **snow**, and ask your child to say the word as Phoneme Fred would say it.

◆ Repeat this for words that rhyme with **snow**.

Step 5: Read the word

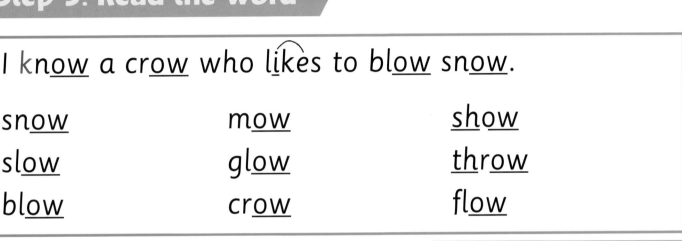

I kn<u>ow</u> a cr<u>ow</u> who likes to bl<u>ow</u> sn<u>ow</u>.

sn<u>ow</u>	m<u>ow</u>	sh<u>ow</u>
sl<u>ow</u>	gl<u>ow</u>	thr<u>ow</u>
bl<u>ow</u>	cr<u>ow</u>	fl<u>ow</u>

◆ Read the sentence at the top of the box with your child.

> Ask your child to exaggerate the *ow* sound as he says the word.

◆ Point to the word **snow**. Say: Read this word so that Phoneme Fred can understand it.

◆ When your child has said the sounds **s-n-ow**, ask: What is the word?

◆ Choose other words for your child to read.

◆ Read each of these words to your child.
Ask him to tell you the sound that the grapheme **o** is making.

go	so	no

Step 6: Spell the word

◆ Choose words from the first box. Say:

> Read this word so that Phoneme Fred can understand it.
> Write the word.

◆ Ask your child to underline each grapheme: <u>s</u> <u>n</u> <u>ow</u>

Step 1: Find the rhyming words

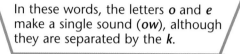

◆ Help your child to think of words that rhyme with **smoke**. Say the words together:

> *joke broke poke choke stoke woke stroke spoke*

◆ Say this rhyming sentence:

> Poke the fire to make it smoke.

> In these words, the letters **o** and **e** make a single sound (**ow**), although they are separated by the **k**.

Step 2: Find the sounds

◆ Play Phoneme Fingers. Say each of the **oke** words with your child, counting the phonemes on your fingers:

> *j-o-k e   p-o-k e   ch-o-k e   w-o-k e*   (3 phonemes)

> *s-m-o-k e   b-r-o-k e   s-t-o-k e   s-p-o-k e*   (4 phonemes)

> *s-t-r-o-k e*   (5 phonemes)

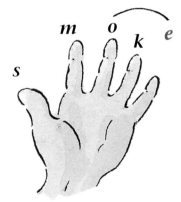

Step 3: Blend the sounds

◆ Say:

> Phoneme Fred is trying to say this word: *s-m-o-k e*
> What is the word?

◆ Repeat this for words that rhyme with **smoke**.

Step 4: Split the word into sounds

◆ Say *smoke*, and ask your child to say the word as Phoneme Fred would say it.

◆ Repeat this for words that rhyme with *smoke*.

Step 5: Read the word

Point out the line joining the *o* to the *e* in each word. Tell your child that they are holding hands.

Poke the fire to make it smoke.

joke	note	stone	hole
poke	wrote	throne	mole
smoke	vote	phone	stole
nose	home	hope	code
rose	gnome	rope	rode
hose	dome	slope	mode

◆ Read the sentence at the top of the box with your child.

Ask your child to exaggerate the vowel sound as she says the word.

◆ Point to the word *smoke*. Say: Read this word so that Phoneme Fred can understand it.

◆ When your child has said the sounds *s-m-o-k e*, ask: What is the word?

◆ Choose other words for your child to read, column by column and then at random.

Step 6: Spell the word

◆ Choose words from the box, column by column and then at random. Say:

Read this word so that Phoneme Fred can understand it.
Write the word.

◆ Ask your child to underline each grapheme and to join the *o* to the *e* with a line: s m o k e

ee, oo, ay, a-e, igh, i-e, ow and o-e

◆ Ask your child to read each set of words, emphasising the vowel sound.

sheep	moon	play	cake	night	pine	snow	smoke
sleep	cool	stray	made	light	bite	low	dome
green	boot	bay	game	bright	like	blow	bone
weed	spoon	day	lame	slight	wipe	throw	hole

◆ Tell your child that some of the words already learned have been mixed up.

◆ Ask your child to read each word.

When your child can read the words easily, see how quickly he or she can read them.

like	made	low	dome	play	pine	bright	bay
boot	game	wipe	throw	cool	snow	hole	sleep
light	weed	lame	moon	blow	stray	bone	day
sheep	cake	bite	slight	spoon	green	night	smoke

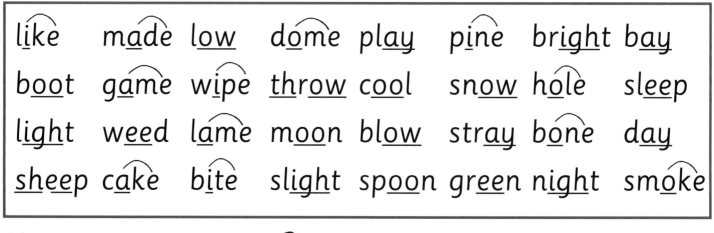

◆ Now help your child to read these verbs (action words).

Show your child how *a-e* verbs, *i-e* verbs and *o-e* verbs drop the *e* before adding *ing*.

| need | needing | needed | sight | sighting | sighted |
| peep | peeping | peeped | slight | slighting | slighted |

| cool | cooling | cooled | hike | hiking | hiked |
| hoot | hooting | hooted | file | filing | filed |

| play | playing | played | glow | glowing | glowed |
| stray | straying | strayed | show | showing | showed |

| tape | taping | taped | stoke | stoking | stoked |
| hate | hating | hated | hope | hoping | hoped |

When *ed* is added to a verb, the ending may be pronounced *d* (taped), *id* (hated) or *t* (liked).

◆ Now help your child to read these plural nouns (naming words). The nouns have been made plural by adding *s*.

| sweets | boots | days | snakes |
| nights | bikes | crows | moles |

◆ Read the following passages with your child.

Words containing graphemes which have not yet been taught are printed in blue. Help your child to read these words by looking at any graphemes which are familiar, and by predicting the words from his or her knowledge of the passage. Teach your child to read *give, have, some* and *you*. (These words are printed without phoneme lines.)

Three sweets

Deepak: Can I have some sw<u>ee</u>ts?

Mum: No, D<u>ee</u>pak.
You have had <u>three</u> pa<u>ck</u>s of sw<u>ee</u>ts tod<u>ay</u>.
You don't n<u>ee</u>d any more.

Deepak: Just give me <u>three</u> sw<u>ee</u>ts!
I f<u>ee</u>l so hungry!

Mum: No, D<u>ee</u>pak. You are t<u>oo</u> gr<u>ee</u>dy!

Deepak: Just give me two sw<u>ee</u>ts!

Mum: No, D<u>ee</u>pak!
Sw<u>ee</u>ts are bad for your t<u>ee</u>th.

Deepak: I wi<u>ll</u> bru<u>sh</u> my t<u>ee</u>th before I go to sl<u>ee</u>p.
Just give me one sw<u>ee</u>t!

Mum: No, D<u>ee</u>pak!
Have a <u>chunk</u> of <u>cheese</u> instead.

Deepak: But I don't l<u>i</u>ke <u>cheese</u>!

Mum: All <u>right</u>. Just one sw<u>ee</u>t!

Off to the moon

"I am off to the moon," said Goon.

"Off to the moon?" said Loon.

"Yes, I am off to the moon, very soon," said Goon.
"I will zoom to the moon with a vroom and a boom!"

"You will need to take some food.
There are no shops on the moon."

"Food?
I won't have room for much food.
I will take a cool green gooseberry fool.
I will sit on a stool and eat gooseberry fool
with a long green spoon, in the gloom, on the moon.
I am off soon.
I am off to the moon!"

So Goon zoomed to the moon!

Vroom! Boom!

Yum, yum!

29

Teach your child to read *was*.

Birthday

Today is here at last!
It seems as if I have been waiting for weeks.

My grandad is coming to stay for my birthday!
I haven't seen him since I was three.
Now I am six. Six today!

My dad and I have baked a fantastic birthday cake.
A thick, gooey chocolate cake in the shape of a rocket!

I stand by the gate and look up and down the street.
My dad says, "He won't come if you keep looking!"

I think of all the games we will play,
and all the things I have to tell him.

I can see a small shape at the end of the street.
It gets closer. It's Grandad!

I run to wake Dad.

"Dad! I can see Grandad!
Grandad is here! Hooray!"

Star light, star bright

"Star light, star bright,
First star I see tonight.
I wish I may, I wish I might
Wish upon a star tonight!"

My mum always sings this song to me on a
clear night, when the sky is bright with moonlight.

I love the sight of the moonlight,
and the smell of the five pine trees on the high,
white cliff.
I love the way the lights flash from the ships
that ride in the bay.

I love to hear my mum
singing the song:

"Star light, star bright,
First star I see tonight.
I wish I may, I wish I might
Wish upon a star tonight!"

Teach your child to read *one* and *would*.

Go home, Jerome

They call him Jerome.
Everyone loves Jerome.
Everyone smiles when they see him.
Everyone laughs when he tells his
long, slow jokes.
Everyone listens when he sings
'Row, row, row your boat', over and over again.

No one woke me from my long dozes
before Jerome came.
No one came to see me in my woodland home.

Now the other gnomes throw snowballs with Jerome,
and my home is filled with smoke from his fire.

Everyone loves Jerome.
I wish he would go home.